EXPLORING OUR OCEANS

ARCTIC OCEAN

by Avery Toolen

pogo

Ideas for Parents and Teachers

Pogo Books let children practice reading informational text while introducing them to nonfiction features such as headings, labels, sidebars, maps, and diagrams, as well as a table of contents, glossary, and index.

Carefully leveled text with a strong photo match offers early fluent readers the support they need to succeed.

Before Reading

- "Walk" through the book and point out the various nonfiction features. Ask the student what purpose each feature serves.
- Look at the glossary together. Read and discuss the words.

Read the Book

- Have the child read the book independently.
- Invite him or her to list questions that arise from reading.

After Reading

- Discuss the child's questions. Talk about how he or she might find answers to those questions.
- Prompt the child to think more. Ask: There is still a lot scientists don't know about the Arctic Ocean. Why do you think this is?

Pogo Books are published by Jump!
5357 Penn Avenue South
Minneapolis, MN 55419
www.jumplibrary.com

Library of Congress Cataloging-in-Publication Data

Names: Toolen, Avery, author.
Title: Arctic Ocean / by Avery Toolen.
Description: Minneapolis, MN: Jump!, Inc., 2023.
Series: Exploring our oceans | Includes index.
Audience: Ages 7-10
Identifiers: LCCN 2021051348 (print)
LCCN 2021051349 (ebook)
ISBN 9781636907680 (hardcover)
ISBN 9781636907697 (paperback)
ISBN 9781636907703 (ebook)
Subjects: LCSH: Arctic Ocean—Juvenile literature.
Classification: LCC GC401 .T66 2023 (print)
LCC GC401 (ebook) | DDC 551.46/132–dc23
LC record available at
https://lccn.loc.gov/2021051348
LC ebook record available at
https://lccn.loc.gov/2021051349

Editor: Jenna Gleisner
Designer: Emma Bersie

Photo Credits: Ondrej Prosicky/Shutterstock, cover (polar bear); Gfed/iStock, cover (seal); jele/Shutterstock, 1; David Havel/Shutterstock, 3; Harvepino/Shutterstock, 4; Naturfoto-Online/Alamy, 5; Thelightwriter/Dreamstime, 6-7; Marian Dreher/Shutterstock, 8-9; All Canada Photos/Alamy, 10; polarman/Shutterstock, 11; FloridaStock/Shutterstock, 12-13; WaterFrame/Alamy, 14-15; imageBROKER/Alamy, 16; RooM the Agency/Alamy, 17; The Picture Art Collection/Alamy, 18-19; U.S. Coast Guard, 20-21; Dolores M. Harvey/Shutterstock, 23.

Printed in the United States of America at Corporate Graphics in North Mankato, Minnesota.

TABLE OF CONTENTS

CHAPTER 1

ICY WATERS

What small but mighty ocean is in the Arctic Circle? It is the Arctic Ocean! Of Earth's five oceans, it is the smallest. It is also the most **shallow**.

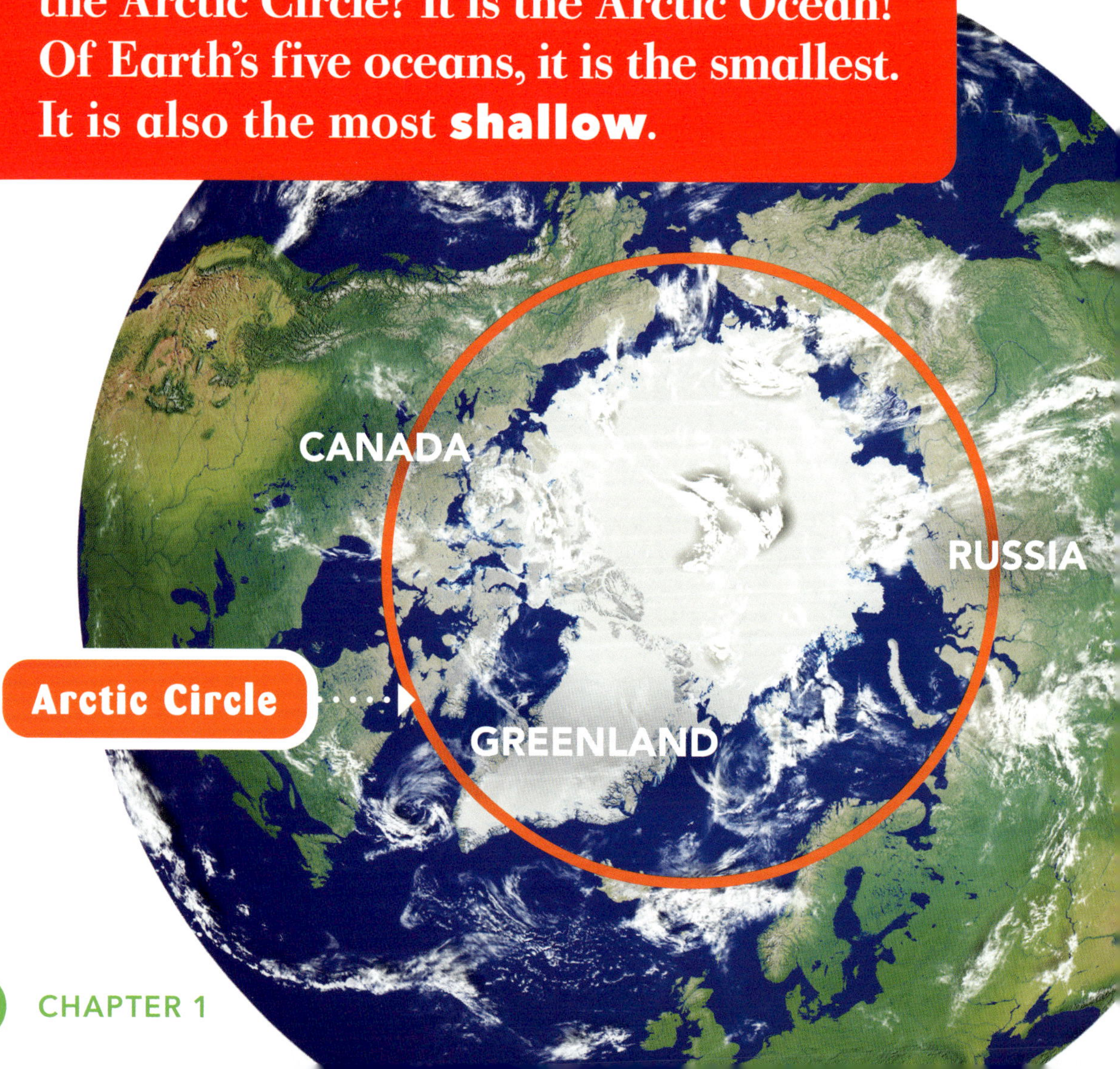

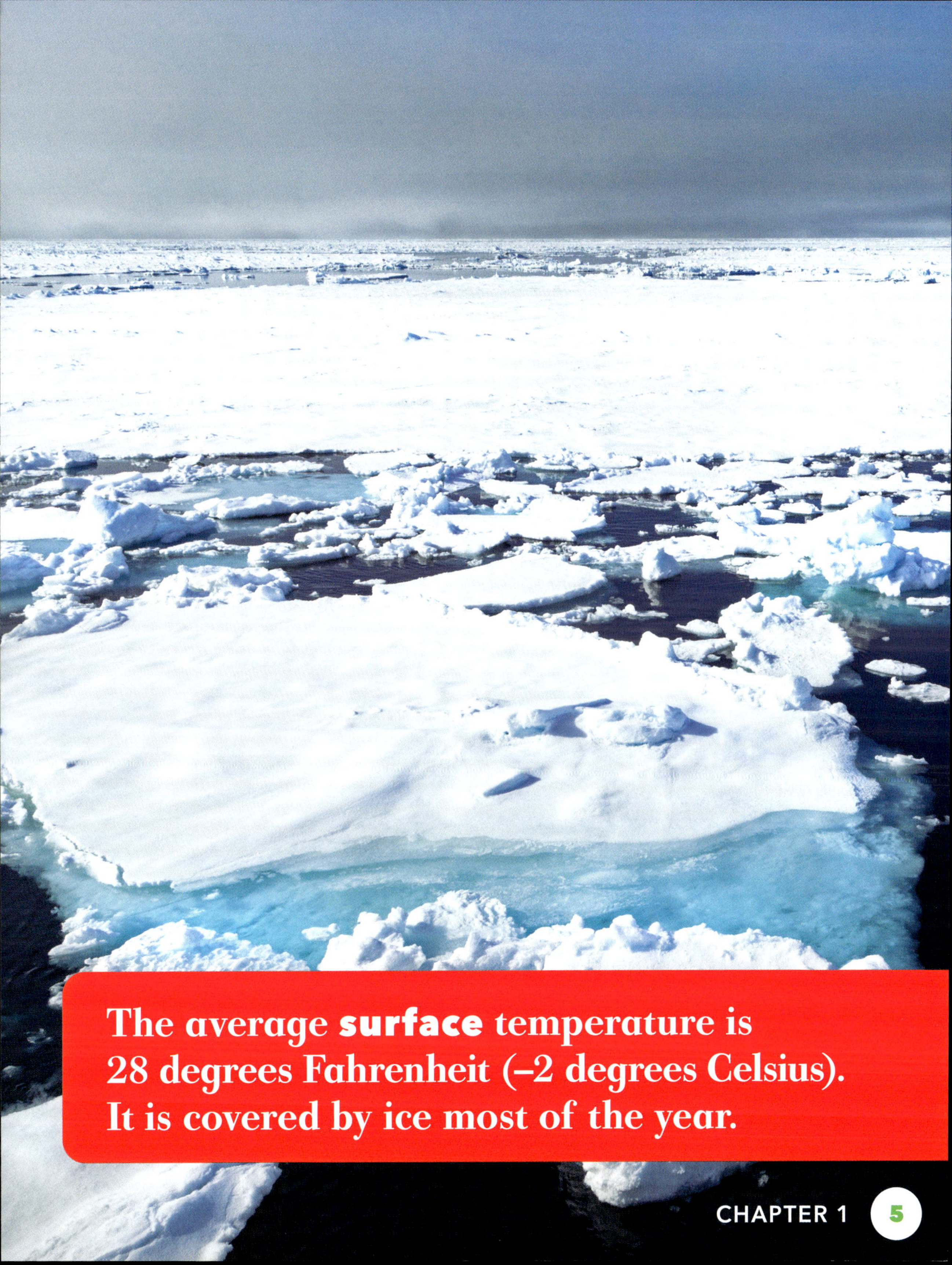

The average **surface** temperature is 28 degrees Fahrenheit (–2 degrees Celsius). It is covered by ice most of the year.

Icebergs float in the water. These big chunks of ice break off of **glaciers**.

TAKE A LOOK!

Where is the Arctic Ocean? Take a look!

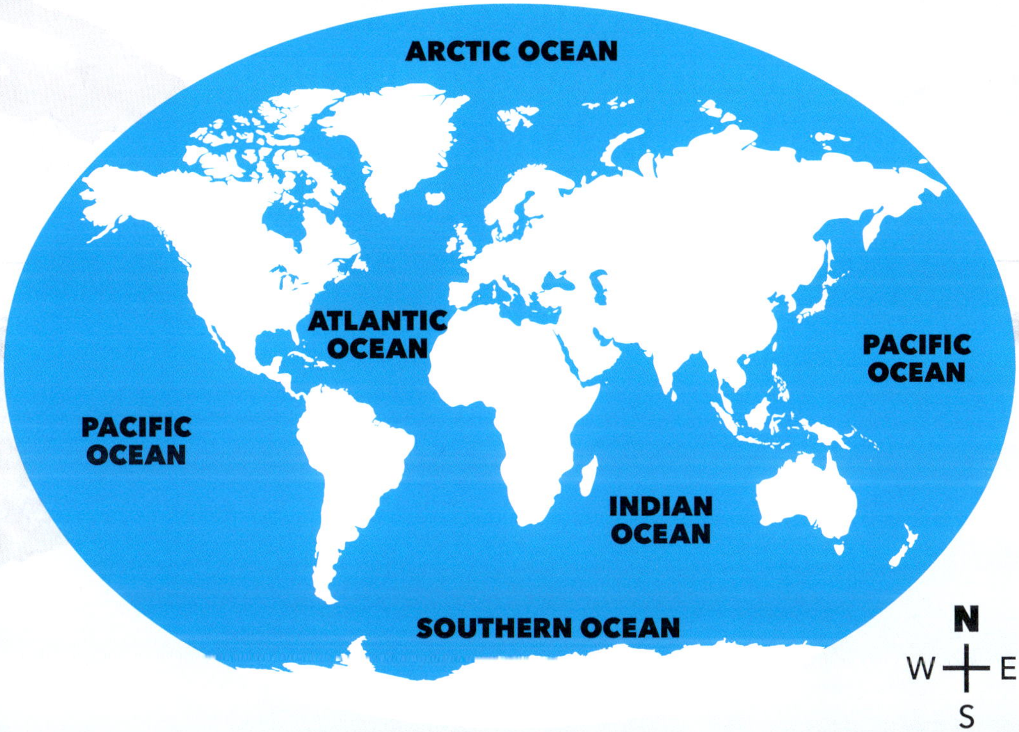

Storms and **ice cover** make it difficult for ships to travel in this ocean. Arctic **cyclones** bring high winds. Big waves break apart sea ice. Cyclones cause warm water to rise to the surface. This melts sea ice. **Climate change** is also melting sea ice.

TAKE A LOOK!

How has ice cover in the Arctic Ocean changed since 1979? Take a look!

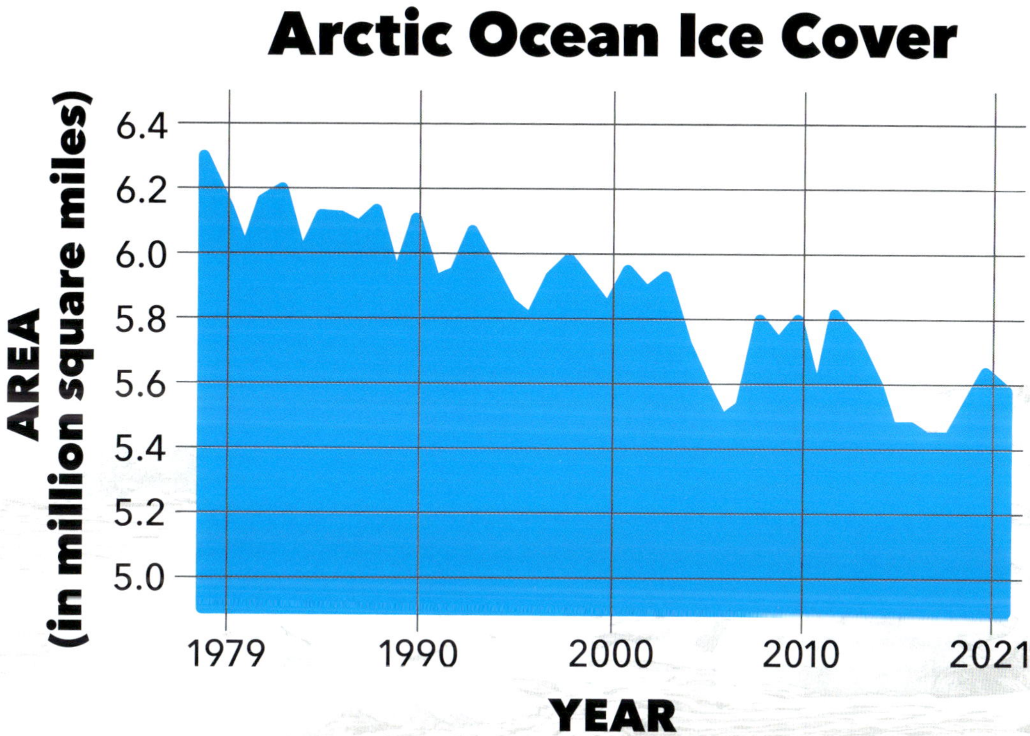

CHAPTER 2

ARCTIC WILDLIFE

Many animals live in the Arctic Ocean. Several whale **species** swim in the icy waters. Narwhals are one. Their tusks can be up to 10 feet (3.0 meters) long!

Several seal species also live here. Ringed seals hunt fish under the sea ice. In spring, females go onto the ice. They give birth to **pups**.

The Arctic is the only place you'll find polar bears. They spend most of their time on sea ice. They hunt, travel, rest, and raise their **cubs** on it.

DID YOU KNOW?

Polar bears and many other Arctic animals are **endangered**. Why? As sea ice melts, it is harder for animals to hunt and raise young.

cub

kelp forest

Many kinds of seaweed also survive the icy waters. Kelp is a kind of seaweed. Kelp forests grow along the Arctic shore. They provide a **habitat** for fish and other sea life.

DID YOU KNOW?

Divers explore many of the world's oceans. Ice makes diving in the Arctic dangerous. Divers wear special gear to stay safe.

CHAPTER 3

EXPLORING THE ARCTIC

Indigenous people explored the Arctic Ocean long before anyone else. They have lived in the Arctic **region** for thousands of years. Some fish in the ocean.

In the 1400s, **explorers** began searching for a Northwest Passage in the Arctic. This route would connect the Atlantic and Pacific Oceans. Storms and sea ice made sailing difficult.

Some ships sank. In 1845, the H.M.S. *Terror* was looking for a Northwest Passage. It got stuck in ice. Eventually, the ship sank. Nobody on the ship was heard from ever again. The ship was found at the bottom of the ocean in 2016.

DID YOU KNOW?

In 1906, Roald Amundsen and his crew were the first to find a Northwest Passage. They came from Norway.

H.M.S. *Terror*

Healy
U.S. COAST GUARD
20

Today, the United States Coast Guard ship *Healy* explores the cold waters. It breaks through the ice. Scientists on the ship map the ocean floor.

The cold and ice make the Arctic Ocean difficult to explore. There is still much to learn about it. What would you like to learn?

ACTIVITIES & TOOLS

TRY THIS!

MELTING SEA ICE

Sea ice is melting in the Arctic. How does this affect polar bears? Find out with this activity.

What You Need:

- five small plastic containers
- water
- freezer
- modeling clay
- one large plastic container

1. **Fill five small plastic containers with about one inch (2.5 centimeters) of water. Put them in the freezer overnight.**
2. **Use modeling clay to sculpt seven to ten polar bears.**
3. **Fill a large plastic container with cold water.**
4. **Take the smaller containers out of the freezer. Ask an adult to help you remove the ice chunks.**
5. **Add the ice chunks to the large plastic container.**
6. **Put your polar bears on the floating chunks of ice.**
7. **Observe them a few times throughout the day. What happens to the ice? Which chunks melt first?**
8. **When one chunk of ice gets too small, move the polar bears to a different one. How does the melting ice impact the polar bears?**

GLOSSARY

climate change: Changes in Earth's weather and climate over time.

cubs: Young polar bears.

cyclones: Storms with very strong winds that rotate and cause damage.

endangered: In danger of becoming extinct, usually because of human activity.

explorers: People who travel in search of geographical or scientific information.

glaciers: Slow-moving masses of ice found in mountain valleys or polar regions.

habitat: A place where a certain animal or plant is usually found.

ice cover: The total area covered by ice.

Indigenous: Of or relating to the earliest known inhabitants of a place.

pups: Young seals.

region: A general area.

shallow: Not deep.

species: One of the groups into which similar animals and plants are divided.

surface: The outermost layer of something.

INDEX

TO LEARN MORE

Finding more information is as easy as 1, 2, 3.

1. Go to www.factsurfer.com
2. Enter "ArcticOcean" into the search box.
3. Choose your book to see a list of websites.